# FUN FOUNDATIONS
# IN WRITING

## By Bonita Lillie

**www.bonitalillie.com**

# D E D I C A T I O N

I dedicate this curriculum to my wonderful fourth grade teacher, Mrs. Kirtley. She recognized the writer within me and coaxed her out onto paper. I am forever grateful!

# Table of Contents

# Note to Parents and Teachers

It's so important for students to start their writing journey on a positive note. From the very beginning, they need to be successful in their writing attempts and, hopefully, find some enjoyment in the process. This curriculum was designed with these goals in mind. *Fun Foundations in Writing* is a gentle step-by-step writing program that introduces students to the fundamentals of writing.

In order to achieve the highest level of success, I believe that students need to be fluent in reading and handwriting before attempting this, or any other writing program. Students who are not yet proficient in these skills can still compose writing that is dictated, but it's my personal recommendation to wait until a student is functioning on at least a fourth grade academic level to begin formal writing instruction. This gives the younger student time to learn important skills such as handwriting, reading, and organized thinking before tackling yet another major skill like writing. It also increases the likelihood that the student will start out with a positive writing experience.

Since this is a beginning writing course, I encourage you, the parent/teacher, to be involved. Make sure your student understands each lesson and is making steady progress. Read what the student writes and evaluate the writing using the lesson evaluation notes on page 66. Let your praises be many and your critiques be few. Most of all, enjoy this journey together!

Disclaimer: All activities mentioned in this book are meant to be performed under adult supervision. Work closely with your student in carrying out the hands-on activities.

# How to Use This Curriculum

Welcome to the world of writing! You are about to start a fun adventure. In this course, I'm going to teach you how to take all of those marvelous thoughts floating around in your imagination and turn them into writing that others can enjoy.

Learning to write is a lot like learning to speak. When you were a young child you learned language from those around you. Little by little, you learned to say words like "Dada" and "Mama". You kept practicing until one day you said big, fancy sentences like, "I want some candy!"

You learn to write the same way you learn to talk. First, someone shows you how to write—that's my job. You start out writing short things, but as you keep practicing you'll be able to write longer pieces. Pretty soon you'll be able to communicate anything that pops into your head.

In this course, you will learn the basic things you need to know in order to write. Each lesson is so simple. This is what you'll do:

1. ☞ Carefully read the key points for each lesson.

2. ✏ Read the writing samples.

3. ✋ Complete the hands-on writing activities listed at the end of each lesson. Your parent or teacher can help you decide which activities to do.

**It's that easy! Why are you waiting? Let's get started!**

# Lesson 1: Writing is Communication

## Goal: Write to communicate.

### Key Points:

☞  Communication means sending and receiving messages.

☞  Writing is a form of communication similar to talking.
Two or more people are involved: the writer and the reader.
Sometimes you will be both.

☞  Writing is putting language on paper in a way that others can
read and understand.

☞  You use writing to express what you think, feel, or know.

☞  The writer and the reader must speak the same language in
order for the reader to understand what is written. For
example, read the writing sample on page 9 and see if you can
understand it. Why or why not?

☞  It's important to write with an audience in mind so
you can write in a way that the audience will
understand. For instance, if you are writing for young
children you can't use big, fancy words.

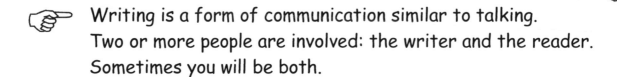

### Writing Sample

Easy to understand:

    *Writing is fun. When you write, you can go to faraway places
like jungles full of tigers, or dark, gloomy castles. You can capture
pirate ships, search for buried treasure, or become a superhero who*

*bravely saves a whole country. You might drive a race car, swim across the ocean, or skydive from a crashing airplane. Writing is a way to do anything, or be anyone. Whatever you can imagine can become real through writing.*

## Difficult to understand:

*Once upon a time a barely mangooth sawticed a neeth. The slinnery neeth beguilted the digeneering catvow and sneeled to a viniscent klab. Plinkering finchlets eggered, "Platooey Platoy!" They skitwelted dadgerdly away. The mangooth caneiced one last time before joggerfooting to a nearby venescu where it bagganiggled forever after.*

## Hands-On Activities

 Read the second paragraph from the writing samples again. This paragraph uses a lot of made-up words. Since no one knows what it really means, decide for yourself and explain the meaning to someone else.

 Discuss with your parent or teacher the following types of communication and how they are used: sign language, musical notes, hieroglyphics, Braille, Morse code, body language, secret codes.

 Observe a pet or animal. Write a list of ways the animal communicates.

 Play a game of Charades. Choose a word and act it out without speaking or writing. Let family or friends try to guess the word. Take turns being the actor and the guessers.

Ask your parent or teacher to help you search online for *Jabberwocky* by Lewis Carroll. Read the poem and see if you can decipher its meaning.

 Sometimes it's fun to create new words that have never been used before. Copy each of the following made-up words on another sheet of paper, and write a definition for each one.
1. Peezlefrump          2. Grafineezing
3. Plawg               4. Gozzamuncher
5. Flinabapper

 Now it's your turn to invent some words. Create five new words and their definitions to add to the five words above. When you are finished, you will have a short dictionary of unusual words.

 Develop secret code words with friends and family. These can be words you make up, or you can use common words to create a code. For example, you might use the word "earplug" to mean, "I'll call you later." Write or type your secret code words and their meanings, and give copies to your friends and family.

 Sometimes words need to be translated from one language to another in order for the reader to understand what is written. Write each of the following words in English, then write each one in another language such as Spanish or French. You might need a parent or teacher to help you locate the new words in a language book or on the Internet. If you know someone who speaks another language, ask that person to help you translate.

| hello | goodbye | car | mother | father |
| house | brother | sister | friend | teacher |
| write | dog | cat | | |

One way to improve communication is to learn new words and increase your vocabulary. Use a dictionary to find five new words you've never seen before. Write each word and its definition on an index card. Throughout the day, try to use the new words in conversation. Challenge friends or family to do the same.

# Lesson 2: Observation Skills

## Goal: Develop observation skills.

### Key Points:

 A writer is an artist who paints pictures with words.

 Writers observe the world around them through their five senses: sight, hearing, smell, touch, and taste.

 Writers see things that others miss. They notice details.

 You must observe things closely before you can pass on your observations to anyone else.

 A writer must make the reader feel like he or she is experiencing the action in the writing.

 In order to be a great writer, you need to develop your observation skills.

### Writing Sample

*Observations of a lemon:*
**Sight**- *It has a bright yellow, bumpy outside. In certain places, the outside looks like it has pores similar to human skin. It has an oval shape with pointed ends. Faint patches of pale green*

12

can be seen, especially at the ends.

**Hearing**- If you drop it on a table it makes a soft thud. When you rub it on your arm it sounds like a quiet swish.

**Smell**- The smell is fresh, clean, and citrus.

**Touch**- The outside feels almost like rubber. It's bumpy, but slick.

**Taste**- The taste is tart, sour, and very strong. It has a tangy, bitter, almost salty flavor.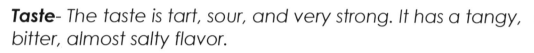

## Hands-On Activities

To complete following activities, go to a place that you like, and get comfortable. Ask your teacher or parent to help you choose which activities to complete.

### Sight

 Play a game of Memory. Choose 20 index cards and make matching pairs by writing the same letter, number, or shape on two cards until you've created 10 pairs. Mix up the cards and turn them face down. Take turns with a friend or family member turning over two cards at a time in an attempt to find matching pairs. If you make a match you get to take another turn. The winner is the person with the most matched sets once all of the cards have been matched.

 Ask a parent or teacher to place 20 items on a tray or table and cover them with a cloth, but don't peek while this is being done. Have the person remove the cloth for one minute while you carefully look at all of the items. After one minute have the person replace the cloth. Write a list of all the items you can remember. When you've finished your list, lift the cloth and see how many you remembered.

Writers notice details that others miss. Ask your parent or teacher to look in the parent/teacher guide for Lesson 2, and ask the questions listed there to see how well you notice things. If you can't answer a lot of the questions, you will need to work on your sight skills.

 Have you ever watched a magic show? Magicians have a saying, "The hand is quicker than the eye." See if you can locate a magician or a magic show in your area. If you are able to watch the magician perform, pay close attention to his hands throughout all the magic tricks that he does. See if you can spot his "trick". If you do discover his secrets, don't ruin the show by saying so. Just keep that knowledge to yourself and know that you're developing great observation skills.

 Set a timer for one minute. Carefully look at everything around you. When the minute is over, write down the things you saw. Without peeking, record as many things as possible.

### Hearing
 Listen to classical music and try to identify the instruments being played. Make a list of the different instruments that you hear. Do the same thing with some of your favorite songs.

 Listen to a variety of types of music and think about the sounds you hear. Does the music put you in a certain mood? Other than the radio or a music player, where might you hear this particular type of music? For example, a lullaby might make you feel sleepy, secure, and comfortable. A place where you might hear this type of music is in a nursery.

 Ask some friends or family members to help you play the

restaurant game. Pretend you are a waiter or waitress attempting to remember a very long order. Take turns naming something to add to the order by going through the alphabet. For example, the first person might order artichokes. The next person would repeat what the first person ordered and then add their own order using the next letter in the alphabet. That person might say artichokes and baked beans. Take turns repeating the entire list and adding a food that begins with the next letter of the alphabet. It might sound like this: artichokes, baked beans, chili, dandelion greens, éclairs...

 Close your eyes or sit blindfolded, and listen to a conversation. What can you tell about the people speaking? Do you know if they are male or female? Can you tell where they are from or their ethnic background? What emotions are they feeling? Are they excited? Happy? Surprised? Sad? Bored? Can you tell their ages, hobbies, interests, or occupations? After you've listened to a conversation, write your observations and discuss them with your parent or teacher.

 Gather your family or friends and play a game of tag, blindfolding the person who is "it". The person who is "it" will attempt to locate and tag the other players simply by following the sound of their voices as they call out. A similar game called Marco Polo can be played in a pool. Make sure that you play in a safe place with adult supervision.

 Set a timer for one minute. Close your eyes and concentrate on what you hear. When the minute is over, write down all the things you heard.

### Smell

  Spices offer a wide variety of smells. Choose several spices from your kitchen, preferably ones that are unfamiliar to you. Smell each one and describe the smell. Use specific words. Does it remind you of anything?

 Go through your house and yard and list as many different smells as you can locate.

 For this exercise, you will need to be blindfolded. Ask your parent or teacher to gather things that have unique smells. A list of ideas is available in the parent/teacher section. While you are blindfolded, smell each item and see if you can identify it. Does the smell remind you of anything? For example, a stinky sock might remind you of a locker room. Hopefully, it wouldn't remind you of your bedroom!

 Set a timer for one minute. Close your eyes and focus on smells. Even if you aren't in a place with strong smells, you should smell something. After a minute, write about the smells using descriptive words.

### Touch

  For this activity, your parent or teacher will blindfold you and give you a variety of objects to feel. A list of ideas is available in the parent/teacher section. Try to identify each object using only your sense of touch.

  Ask your parent/teacher to assemble several items of clothing while you are blindfolded. A list of ideas is available in the parent/teacher section. Feel the

different textures and fabrics. For each item, answer the following questions.

1. Would you wear this in winter, spring, summer, or autumn? Why did you choose that season?
2. Is this casual, something you would wear around the house, or something you would wear to a formal occasion? How can you tell?
3. Is this item worn by a man or woman? Why?
4. Would this be comfortable or uncomfortable to wear? Explain your answer.

 Goop is a really cool substance that will stimulate your sense of touch. To make it, combine a box of cornstarch with  one cup of water. Mix until all the dry ingredients are wet. You may need to add a small amount of extra water, but not much or it will ruin the texture of the goop. Sink your hands into the goop and play with it. Discuss the following questions with your parent/teacher.

1. What does goop feel like when you touch the surface of it?
2. How does it feel when you sink your hands into it?
3. Grab a handful of goop and let it drip from your fingers. How does it feel?
4. Place a small amount on wax paper or a hard surface and let it dry. What does it feel like after it's dried?
5. Does goop feel like anything else you've touched before? If so, what was it?

 Set a timer for one minute. Close your eyes and pay attention to what you feel. Think about the temperature, what you're sitting on, your clothes. How do things feel? After a minute, write your observations about the things you felt.

## Taste

Your sense of taste and your sense of smell are closely linked, and if you can't smell you might have a hard time tasting. Choose some foods with strong flavors and some that are mild. Use your fingers or a clothespin to pinch your nose as you sample each food. Were you able to taste the food? Which ones? Did the food taste differently than it normally does? Discuss your observations with your parent/teacher.

Cooks use a lot of spices to make more foods tasty. Gather some spices and smell them one by one. As you smell each one, make a list of foods which you think that spice would be used to season. When you are finished, look through a cookbook or ask your parent/teacher to help you locate information about those spices on the Internet, and see if your guesses are correct.

Saliva is also a very important part of tasting. Assemble a variety of foods with different flavors, such as something sweet, something salty, something sour, and something bland. Use a paper towel to completely dry your tongue. Immediately after drying your tongue, before you draw it back into your mouth, place a piece of food on it. Can you taste it? Does it have a different taste than usual? Dry your tongue thoroughly again and try another food. Keep drying your tongue and testing the different kinds of food to see if you can taste them.

In order to do this activity, you will need to wear a blindfold. Ask a family member or friend to choose several foods for you to taste. As you taste each one, think about words which describe that taste. You may want to guess what you are tasting, too. When the blindfold is removed, write the words you used to describe the tastes you experienced.

# Lesson 3: Words

> **Goal:** Use a variety of words to communicate in writing.

## Key Points:

☞ Writing starts with words because words are the building blocks of language.

☞ It takes many different types of words to communicate through writing.

☞ Always use the most specific words possible to paint vivid pictures in the reader's mind.

☞ A noun is a word which represents a person, place, thing, or idea. Nouns are words that answer the questions: Who? What? Where? See examples on page 21.

boy

☞ Plural means more than one, so a plural noun is a noun that isn't alone. It's more than one of the same thing. See examples on page 21.

boys

☞ A proper noun gives a name to a noun. See examples on page 21.

John

☞ A verb is an action word. Without verbs, nouns don't know what to do. Verbs add excitement and adventure to writing. See examples on page 21.

☞ Modifiers are words which change other words or make them more clear:

<u>Adjectives</u> are describing words which change nouns.
(See examples on this page.)

<u>Adverbs</u> are modifiers which change verbs.
(See examples on this page.)

## <u>Writing Sample</u>

<u>Nouns</u>:  gorilla, gum, bug, javelin, democracy, tunnel

<u>Plural noun</u>:  asteroids, daisies, sledgehammers, pancakes, clowns, dollars

<u>Proper noun</u>:  Mr. Smellybreath, The Sour Stomach Café, Rabbitville, Bigfoot

<u>Verb</u>:  whine, gobble, yodel, spit, dangle, dive

<u>Adjective</u>:  <u>smelly</u> socks, <u>tie-dyed</u> hair, <u>gooey</u> toe cheese, <u>frantic</u> shopper, <u>fresh</u> roadkill

<u>Adverb</u>:  eat <u>fast</u>, snore <u>loudly</u>, clean <u>wildly</u>, growl <u>dangerously</u>

## <u>Hands-On Activities</u>

<u>Nouns</u>
Without moving from where you are,
name as many nouns as you see around you.

Some nouns are very general, and others are specific. On a separate piece of paper, change each of the general nouns below into a specific noun.

Example:   General noun: book
Specific noun: diary

General nouns:

| money | hat | candy | beverage | pet |
|-------|-----|-------|----------|-----|
| job | color | season | fruit | sport |

 Write the letters of your name down the left margin of a piece of notebook paper. For each letter, write a noun that represents you.

Example:   B-boy
O-outfielder
B-brother

## Plural Nouns

Most nouns are turned into plural nouns simply by adding an "s" to the end of the word. For example, a *friend* becomes *friends* and *car* becomes *cars*. However, some nouns have unusual plural forms. Write the following list of nouns on a separate paper. Beside each noun write the word that you think is the plural of that noun.  Check your answers with your parent or teacher.

| child | ox | mouse | foot |
|-------|-----|-------|------|
| goose | mongoose | tooth | man |
| woman | sheep | deer | moose |
| baby | city | potato | hero |
| box | life | half | loaf |
| wolf | person | cactus | |

## Proper Nouns

As we said in an earlier assignment, some nouns are general and some are specific. A proper noun is very specific and actually gives a name to a noun. On a separate piece of paper, change each of the following general nouns to proper nouns.

Example:

General noun: holiday

Specific noun: Thanksgiving

General nouns:

| | | | | |
|---|---|---|---|---|
| dog | state | tree | month | song |
| teacher | friend | president | place | book |

Write proper nouns to answer each of these questions:
1. What are the full names of each member of your family?
2. What are your pets' names?
3. What is your favorite book?
4. What is your favorite movie?
5. What is your favorite song?
6. What is the name of your favorite store?
7. What is the name of your favorite restaurant?
8. What are the names of your doctor and your dentist?
9. What is the name of the street where you live?
10. What is the name of your school?

## Adjectives

Write the letters of your name down the left margin of a piece of notebook paper. For each letter, write an adjective that describes you.

Example:     B- bold

O-outgoing

B-bossy

Play the restaurant game with a friend or family member. Pretend you are a waiter or waitress trying to remember a long order without writing it down on paper. The first person should order something that has an adjective starting with an "a" For example, that person might order "awesome apples". The second person repeats what the first person said and adds a new order beginning with the next letter of the alphabet. For example, that person might say "awesome apples and bountiful blueberries". Continue the game using each letter of the alphabet to add a new food with an adjective that describes it.

Choose a magazine picture and list as many adjectives as you can that describe the picture.

Write the following nouns on a piece of paper, and add adjectives to describe them:

1. pizza          3. firecracker
2. monster        4. toy

## Verbs

Let's play the verb game. Get together with friends or family members. One person calls out an action that each person has to perform. For example, the first person might say, "Pat your head." The players pat their heads and continue to do so. The next person calls out another action, and all players perform it while continuing to do the first action, too. For example, while everyone is patting his or her head, the second player might say, "March in place." Each player calls out a new action, and all players try to do the new action while continuing to perform all of the other actions that have been given. See how many actions you can perform at one time. This game can be really challenging and funny.

Choose a magazine picture. List all of the actions you see taking place in the picture. Don't just list the obvious ones. Really think about everything that is happening.

 For one minute, perform as many actions as you possibly can. For example, stand up, sit down, hop, skip, jump, smile, shake, giggle, wiggle, and wink. When the minute is over, write the actions you performed. If a friend or family member is nearby, compete to see who can perform the most actions in a single minute.

Adverbs

 Play the verb game on page 23 again. Only this time add an adverb to each action. For example, you might say, "Pat your head <u>slowly</u>" or "Sing the national anthem <u>loudly</u>."

 Now that you know some of the different types of words used in writing, let's do a fun writing exercise. In the parent/teacher section of this book I've written two paragraphs that are missing a few words. Your job is to fill in the missing words without knowing the subject of each paragraph. Your parent or teacher will ask you for different parts of speech such as a noun or a verb. Be as creative as possible with your answers. When all the blanks in the paragraph have been filled your parent or teacher will read the paragraph to you. It will likely sound very funny.

 Write these verbs on a piece of paper and add adverbs to change them:

    1. dance
    2. laugh
    3. yell
    4. drive

# Lesson 4: Basic Sentence Structure

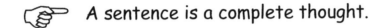

| Goal: Write using complete sentences. |
| --- |

## Key Points:

☞ A sentence is a complete thought.

☞ Every sentence begins with a capital letter and ends with a punctuation mark.

| . ? ! |
| --- |

☞ The subject of a sentence tells who or what is doing something. I like to call it the do-er or the be-er. See examples on page 27.

☞ The verb is the action the subject takes. See examples on page 27.

☞ The simplest sentences have only two words: one subject and one verb. Read these examples:

1. Caroline cheers.          3. Ben slept.
2. Jody skates.               4. Rover hid.

☞ A sentence fragment is not a complete sentence. It is missing the subject, or verb, or both. See examples on page 27.

☞ A run-on sentence is really two or more sentences joined together, but they are two complete thoughts that need to be made into two separate sentences. Sometimes there are more than two. See examples on page 27.

## Writing Sample

*Subjects:*
1. <u>My dog </u>ate my homework.
2. <u>Jim </u>enjoys playing football.
3. <u>A tornado </u>destroys things.

*Verbs:*
1. Edgar <u>burps </u>after every meal.
2. Jennie <u>bounced </u>around like a kangaroo.
3. Joe's uncle <u>whittles </u>wood into whistles.

*Sentence Fragments:*
1. and was never seen again
2. ran after the cat
3. several of the most talkative students

*Run-on sentences:*
1. Mike is a farmer he likes to grow plants.
2. Rex hates the meter reader he barks and tries to bite him.
3. I'm taking a writing course it's fun I like to write.


# Hands-On Activities

 On a separate piece of paper, turn each fragment from the writing sample into a complete sentence. Don't forget to capitalize the first letter and add punctuation.

 In the writing sample, you also read some run-on sentences. On a separate piece of paper, divide those run-on sentences into sentences that express a single thought.

 Write each of the following words on index cards or individual pieces of paper:

|  |  |  |  |
|---|---|---|---|
| the | speedy | red | race |
| car | chased | the | yellow |
| convertible | sports | car |  |

Rearrange the words above to make as many different sentences as possible. You will need to write each sentence in order to keep track of how many you create. These words can make a lot of sentences, so you might need to work on this project over several days. I'll get you started with this sentence:

| the | speedy | red | race | car | chased | the | yellow | convertible | sports | car |
|---|---|---|---|---|---|---|---|---|---|---|

 Once you've created as many sentences as possible, turn to page 69 to see how many I wrote.

 Read the following paragraph and discuss with your parent or teacher what's missing or what's wrong.

*dogs make great pets you can train them to do tricks they can go on walks with you they guard your house dogs are loyal to their owners a dog is a man's best friend*

Do you see why sentences are important? Break the paragraph into individual sentences and write each one on a separate line. Be sure to capitalize each sentence and end each one with a punctuation mark.

 The following sentences are missing subjects. On a separate piece of paper write the sentences, adding a subject to each one. Be creative. It's okay to make funny sentences.

1. _____ drinks chocolate milk.
2. _____ rises at 5:00 a.m. and crows.

3. _____ is the best idea in the world.
4. _____ is a champion tree climber.
5. _____ likes chubby puppies and skinny lizards.

The following sentences are missing verbs. On a separate piece of paper write the following sentences, adding a verb to each one. Remember to think creatively.

1. The giant gorilla _____.
2. My sister's hair _____.
3. The magician_____.
4. My mother's cousin's nephew's son _____.
5. My dad's old jalopy car _____.

Look at what's happening around you at this moment. Write five sentences that tell what is happening, but use only two words per sentence - one subject and one verb.

# Lesson 5: Declarative Sentences

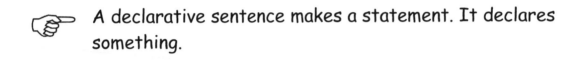

## Goal: Write declarative sentences.

## Key Points:

☞ A declarative sentence makes a statement. It declares something.

☞ It may state a fact or facts.

☞ A declarative sentence can also state an opinion.

☞ A declarative sentence isn't always a true statement. A false statement can also be a declarative sentence.

☞ Declarative sentences usually end with a period.  .

## Writing Sample

*Facts:*
*1. Puppies become dogs.*
*2. Kittens become cats.*
*3. Tadpoles do not become flagpoles.*

*Opinions:*
*1. Tiny green aliens from outer space are scary.*
*2. Spinach tastes great.*
*3. Roses smell gross.*

*True Statements:*
*1. We live on earth.*

2. *People breathe air.*
3. *The sun comes up in the morning.*

*False Statements:*
1. *Brown cows make chocolate milk.*
2. *Grasshoppers rule the world.*
3. *I saw a T-Rex walking down my street yesterday.*

## Hands-On Activities

 Listen to a conversation around you or on television. Count how many declarative sentences you hear.

 Read a page from a favorite book. Locate and count all of the declarative sentences on that page.

 You know yourself better than anyone else. Write five statements about yourself.

 Think about your best friend. Write five sentences stating the things you most like about your friend.

 Weather forecasters use a lot of declarative sentences in their weather reports. Pretend you are a weather forecaster. Prepare a weather report for your area by listing 5-10 statements about your current weather and what to expect in days to come. Give the weather report orally for family or friends. Use maps or anything else you need to make it seem as real as possible.

 Pretend you are the host of an animal show, and you are reporting about a new creature that has been discovered deep in the Amazon jungle. Write at least five statements about the creature. Feel free to draw a picture of this new creature, too. Present your findings as if you are the host of the animal show.

 Sometimes news reporters ask people to give statements about current events. Look through a newspaper and find a story about an interesting current event. Pretend the reporter has asked for your opinion on this topic. Write your opinion using at least three declarative sentences.

 Write five declarative sentences about things that you like.

# Lesson 6: Imperative Sentences

Goal: Write imperative sentences.

## Key Points:

 An imperative sentence gives a command or instruction. That doesn't mean you have to yell. An imperative sentence simply tells someone what to do.

 Like other sentences, imperative sentences begin with a capital letter and end with a punctuation mark.

 An imperative sentence can end with a period or an exclamation point.

. or !

## Writing Sample

*Simon says:*
*Jump up and down.*
*Bend over and touch your toes.*
*Pat your head and rub your belly at the same time.*
*Stick your tongue out and put your fingers in your ears.*
*Shake your head.*
*Waddle like a duck.*
*Moo like a cow.*
*Strut like a rooster.*
*Pretend you're a penguin.*
*March to the left.*
*March to the right.*
*Sit down.*
*Complete the hands-on activities for this lesson.*

## Hands-On Activities

 Parents use a lot of imperative sentences. Listen throughout the day and write some of the commands your parents give.

 Play a game of Simon Says and give really goofy commands.

 Have you ever tried to teach tricks to a dog? Think about what you would say to a dog if you were a trainer. Write at least five imperative sentences commanding the dog to perform a task or a trick. If you have a dog for a pet, try training the dog to follow the commands in your imperative sentences. It might take time, patience, and doggy treats to get the job done, but it's fun.

 Pretend you are a police officer in hot pursuit of a suspect in a crime. What commands would you yell at the suspect? Write all of those commands.

 Soldiers, especially new soldiers who are being trained in boot camp, hear lots of imperative sentences from their commanding officers If you were a military drill sergeant, what commands might you give to the soldiers in training? Write your commands.

 Doctors use a lot of imperative sentences. Think of orders a doctor might give to a sick patient, and write at least five of them.

 If you like reading science fiction, you are probably very familiar with spaceships. Pretend you're a space-ship commander and your ship is about to land on a

planet that no one has ever visited. What orders might you give to your crew before they step out of the ship? Write your orders on a separate piece of paper so the crew will have a copy to take with them.

 Have you ever used a self-checkout cash register at a store? Those machines can be quite bossy. List all of the commands you remember hearing from a self-checkout machine.

 If you could tell anyone to do anything, what five commands would you give? Write them on a piece of paper.

# Lesson 7: Interrogative Sentences

## Goal: Use interrogative sentences.

### Key Points:

 An interrogative sentence asks a question.

 It ends with a question mark.   **?**

 Some interrogative sentences begin with words like *who, what, when, where, why, which,* and *how.*

 Like other sentences, an interrogative sentence begins with a capital letter.

### Writing Sample

*What would you do if you were president?*
*Which way did that huge pink rhinoceros go?*
*Who invented skateboards?*
*How can I get my sister to do my chores for a penny?*
*Why can't chocolate be as good for you as broccoli?*
*When will I ever be grown up?*
*Where is my favorite piece of already-chewed gum?*
*Does your pet rock do tricks?*
*If I make weird faces, will my face really freeze that way?*
*Have you ever flown on a flying trapeze?*
*Did my parents really walk uphill to school and uphill back home again every day for twelve years?*

## Hands-On Activities

  Listen to a conversation around you or on television. Count the number of questions asked.

  Pretend you are a reporter getting ready to interview someone you know. Write questions you would use in your interview. If you want to take it a step further, use your questions and interview the person.

 If you ever work as a waitress or waiter you will ask a lot of questions. You can practice this skill by serving your family during a meal. Choose a meal, and be the waiter or waitress for your family. Ask the same questions you would ask if you were working in a restaurant. After the meal your family can help you remember the questions that you asked. Write them on paper.

 If you hadn't seen a close friend in a very long time, you would have some catching up to do. What types of questions would you ask each other? Write at least five questions that you would ask your friend.

  Animals don't speak, but what if they did? If animals were given the ability to speak for just one afternoon, what questions would you ask your pet or another animal? Make a list of those interrogative sentences.

 What if you got a once in a lifetime opportunity to meet your favorite celebrity? What questions would you ask? Think about those questions, and then write them on paper. You might actually get the chance to meet that person one day, and you will be glad you prepared ahead of time.

It's reported that a life form from another galaxy has landed on earth, and you are the person chosen to interview this being. What are the important things earthlings need to know?  Think very carefully, and write the list of interrogative sentences you will ask when you conduct your interview on prime time television.

# Lesson 8: Exclamatory Sentences

Goal: Write exclamatory sentences.

## Key Points:

 Exclamatory sentences express a lot of excitement or emotion.

An exclamatory sentence ends with an exclamation point. | ! |

An exclamatory sentence can make a statement like a declarative sentence.

An exclamatory sentence doesn't give a command. That would be an imperative sentence even if it ends with an exclamation point.

Don't overuse exclamatory sentences or exclamation points.

## Writing Sample

*I'm so excited!*
*That's hilarious!*
*You won!*
*I can't wait!*
*This is crazy!*

# Hands-On Activities

 Exclamatory sentences aren't necessarily used every day. Make a point today to take note of any exclamatory sentences that you hear.

 Ask your family to spend an hour talking to one another only in exclamatory sentences. What do you notice about the noise level? How does this affect the mood of your family? Why do you think exclamatory sentences are only used occasionally?

 What if we never used exclamatory sentences? Spend an hour or so talking with your family in flat voices without expressing emotions. What would life be like if everyone spoke that way all the time? Why do you think exclamatory sentences are important?

 Pretend you just got elected to be head cheerleader of the cheerleading squad and you have to write the first cheer of the season. Write a cheer using exclamatory sentences that will be sure to spur your team to victory.

 Make a list of exclamatory sentences that you might yell to the players on your team if they were in the World Series. What would you say to make them want to win the game?

 You're a fireman who just entered a burning building to save people. What messages of hope might you yell to those in the building as you find your way to them? Write a list of exclamatory sentences expressing what you would say.

You just won a million dollars! What do you have to say about that? Write the exclamatory sentences you might say if you actually did win that much money.

# Lesson 9 Paragraph Formation

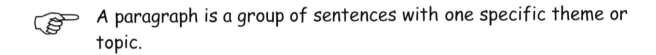

**Goal: Write a paragraph.**

## Key Points:

☞ A paragraph is a group of sentences with one specific theme or topic.

☞ A paragraph needs a topic sentence that tells the subject of the paragraph.

☞ Paragraphs also have supporting sentences that give the details of the topic.

☞ A paragraph is like an island. It can stand alone or be grouped with other paragraphs to form longer pieces of writing.

☞ Paragraphs are indented. That is how you tell where one paragraph ends and another begins.

## Writing Samples

#1    *This is an island. It has sandy beaches, and it's surrounded by water. Palm trees and tropical plants grow here. It even has tasty island fruits. Yes, this is an island and we'll probably be stranded here for the rest of our lives.*

#2    *Have you seen my lost pet? He's rather large, about 10 stories high. He has a giant mouth and fierce, sharp teeth. His skin is dry and scaly and he doesn't like to be petted. When he walks, the ground* shakes and people think an earthquake is happening. He gobbles up pretty much everything in sight. If you happen to see him, take cover and call me.

*#3*    If I were invisible, I'd quietly slip out of my house right about the time my mom pulled out the math book. I'd run down the road until I spotted a horse, and I'd jump on his back and ride to the airport. Once I got to the airport, I'd board a plane and fly across the ocean. I'd see new places, like deserts, castles, and tall, treacherous mountains. I'd ride on the backs of lions, hug a giant polar bear, and sit beside a snake charmer as he blew his musical pipe. Yes, if I were invisible I'd go everywhere, see everyone, and do everything—except my math lesson.

## Hands-On Activities

 Look through one of your favorite books. Read a page or two. Notice that each paragraph is indented. How long are the paragraphs? Which ones are especially interesting? Why?

 After you've looked at paragraphs in your favorite book, look at paragraphs in a newspaper. Do you notice any differences between paragraphs in the book and those in the newspaper? Which ones are longer? Which ones are shorter?

 Ask your parent or teacher to help you find a suitable website to view. What do you notice about paragraphs on the Internet? How do they differ from paragraphs in a book or magazine?

 Pretend you've just discovered a new, unusual island that no one has ever seen before. Write a paragraph about it. You will get a lot more practice writing paragraphs in future lessons, but do your best now.

# Lesson 10: The Topic Sentence

## Goal: Write clear topic sentences.

**Key Points:**

☞ The topic sentence tells the subject of the paragraph.

☞ A topic sentence can appear at the beginning, middle, or end of a paragraph, but it's usually at the beginning.

☞ All other sentences in a paragraph must relate to the main subject found in the topic sentence.

☞ When writing a paragraph, make sure the topic isn't too big. For example, don't try to write about all the movie stars in the world in a single paragraph. Pick your favorite and write a few facts about that person.

**Writing Samples**

#1    <u>Ants are hard workers.</u> *They are always moving and doing. They work together in teams to build big ant hills, to gather and store food, and to create more ants. If you stomp on an ant hill, the ants will rush out and quickly attack you. They will also get busy repairing the ant hill right away. Ants get a lot done!*

#2    *The evidence is obvious. He looks weird and acts even stranger. He eats abnormal foods like peanut butter and banana sandwiches, or ketchup on his macaroni and cheese. His feet stink* *and his friends are really odd. The proof is clear: <u>My brother is an alien from outer space.</u>*

*#3    <u>A monster lives in my room.</u> The other night I saw his head moving from side to side in the dark, looking for me. He murmured in a constant whir as if he couldn't speak. Worst of all, I felt his icy breath blowing on me every time he turned my way. I hid under the covers until the next morning when Mom came in to wake me. She turned off my fan and the monster was gone, but I know he'll be back when darkness falls.*

## Hands-On Activities

 Look through a newspaper or magazine. Choose three interesting headlines or article titles. Pretend you have been assigned to write a paragraph about each one. On a separate piece of paper, copy the headlines or article titles, and write the topic sentence you would use for each paragraph.

 The following paragraphs are missing a topic sentence. Please write one for each paragraph.

1. If you continue looking up into a clear night sky for several minutes you will probably spot one, or possibly more than one. It will look like a sudden flash of light that bursts and falls quickly. In a matter of seconds, it will be completely gone. If you have never seen one, it's worth it to keep looking for one because they are spectacular to behold.

2. First, you go up in an airplane with a parachute strapped to your back. When the plane reaches the right height you jump out and free fall for a while. Then you pull the cord and a parachute quickly expands above you as your fall suddenly halts to a fast

glide. You look at the beautiful scenery as you get closer and closer to land.  The landing can be tricky so you have to be careful that you don't suffer an injury as you hit earth. It's so much fun!

3.  You see the most amazing things there. Tigers, lions, and  other wild animals perform in the three middle rings. Acrobats twist themselves into all sorts of shapes. Tight rope walkers and trapeze artists perform overhead. Beautiful ladies in glittering costumes ride elephants around the arena. Clowns perform funny stunts and tricks to make people laugh. Vendors sell buttery popcorn and wispy cotton candy. It's truly the greatest show on earth.

 In the next lesson you will be asked to write a paragraph about yourself. Write the topic sentence for that paragraph now.

# Lesson 11: Supporting Sentences

> Goal: Write sentences that support the topic sentence of a paragraph.

## Key Points:

☞ Each supporting sentence must relate to the topic sentence. It must stay on the same subject as the topic sentence.

☞ Supporting sentences make the topic sentence stronger by adding more information about the topic.

☞ The supporting sentences add details to a paragraph, and often answer the questions: Who? What? When? Where? Why? How?

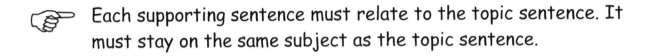

who what
when where
why how

☞ Supporting sentences can be long or short. It's best to use a combination of both types to add variety and to make the paragraph more interesting.

## Writing Samples

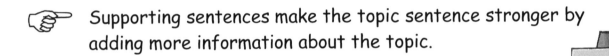

    *I'm Lori and I'm thirteen. Basketball and soccer are my favorite sports. I don't watch them on TV though. If someone asked me what type of food I like, I'd say Mexican enchiladas. I'm homeschooled. My favorite subjects are poetry and social studies. I have three pets: one cat, one puppy, and one dog. My favorite animals are horses. My hobbies are working at a farm with horses and drawing. Recently, I started playing the lap harp. My favorite colors are purple, orange, and blue. What I like to do in my spare time is write in my journal and play with my puppy. Also, I like to play on the*

*computer. My talents are probably dancing and riding horses. That's all about me.*

*Lori L. - age 13*

*My name is Breanne and I'm a ten year old tomboy. I enjoy playing softball and beating up boys. I also like drama and sewing. I am a true southerner, but my favorite baseball team is the Boston Red Sox. I love reading and writing, when I'm in the right mood.*

*Breanne L. - age 10*

## Hands-On Activities

 Create a paragraph for each topic sentence below by adding supporting sentences. Feel free to use your imagination in creating these paragraphs.

1. You can have a lot of fun on a rainy day.
2. A strange thing happened the other day.
3. When I grow up I'm going to do something really special.
4. It's easy to make your own disguises.

 Make a short list of interesting things about you. If someone had never met you before, what might they want to know? If you need help coming up with ideas, talk it over with a family member.

| Me |
|---|
| 1. |
| 2. |
| 3. |
| 4. |
| 5. |
| 6. |

 Using the topic sentence you wrote in Lesson 10 and the list you made about yourself in the previous activity, write a paragraph about you. It should be at least six sentences in length.

# Lesson 12: Expository Paragraphs

> ## Goal: Write an expository paragraph.

## Key Points:

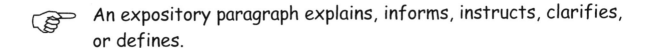

- 👉 An expository paragraph explains, informs, instructs, clarifies, or defines.

- 👉 An expository paragraph usually contains a lot of facts, but may also include opinions.

- 👉 Expository paragraphs use a lot of declarative sentences. (See Lesson 5.)

- 👉 You can't tell everything there is to know about a subject in one expository paragraph, so choose a narrow topic. Example: Instead of writing about every pet you've ever owned, choose one pet per paragraph.

## Writing Samples

*#1    I enjoy making whipped cream pies.  First, you need to get together with a friend.  Gather two pie pans and two cans of whipped cream.  Fill your pans with whipped cream, being sure to get some on your fingers so you have to lick it off.  Once the pans are full, take a moment to admire your lovely creations before you smash them in each other's faces. Your face will be very yummy!*

*B.L.*

*\*\*Please get your parent's permission before making whipped cream pies.*

*#2    The definition of a true friend is someone who is always there for you. On your good days, the friend is there to enjoy them with you. When things aren't going well or you're feeling blue, your friend will cheer you up and lift your spirits, or cry with you if necessary. When you make mistakes or embarrass yourself or someone else, a true friend won't make you feel bad. A real friend will still like you, and might even help you laugh about it. True friends will always have you with them in their hearts.*                                    *B.L.*

*#3    Science is my favorite subject. I like discovering new things and experimenting. My favorite topic is learning about spacecraft and the planets, how they orbit the sun. On my perfect home school day, my dad would take me to the planetarium to watch shows about the planets and stars. After we returned from the planetarium, we would do an experiment on how the planets orbit the sun.*
                                    *Madeline L. - age 12*

## Hands-On Activities

 Everyone, including you, is an expert on something. Interview family members and friends.  Ask them what they think you're good at and what subjects you know well. Make a list of their answers.

 Choose one of the things from the previous activity that you know well or are good at, and write a list of statements or facts about that topic.

 Look at your list of expert topics from the previous activity and write an expository paragraph that gives information about one of the topics that you know well.

Write an expository paragraph explaining how to play your favorite game.

 Choose a vocabulary word or an unusual word from the dictionary. Write a paragraph that defines the word. Instead of copying the meaning from the dictionary, write it in your own words and write your own examples to show how the word might be used in language.

# Lesson 13: Narrative Paragraphs

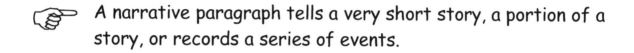

## Goal: Write a narrative paragraph.

## Key Points:

☞ A narrative paragraph tells a very short story, a portion of a story, or records a series of events.

☞ A narrative paragraph can be about a real or imaginary topic.

☞ Narrative paragraphs use a lot of declarative sentences. (See Lesson 5.)

☞ Don't try to write a book in a single narrative paragraph. Write about one specific thing or event.

☞ When writing a narrative paragraph, it's important to keep the events in the right order. This is called sequencing.

| First |
|-------|
| Second |
| Third |

## Writing Sample

On a bright, sunny day a little wide-eyed, brown-haired eight-year-old girl was holding her mother's hand while walking to the market. On the way, a golden glimmer caught her eye from the sidewalk. She examined it more closely to see what it was. It was a coin with three stars on the back and a hole through the top where it was used for a charm. She stooped down and picked it up. The three stars looked familiar. Maggie had seen these stars before on something, and had asked her mother about it. She remembered she had seen it on a mailbox on Graceway Street, which is near the *market. She asked her mother if they could go to that house to see if the owner of the house was also the owner of the coin.*

*Elise G. - age 11*


*Today was a busy day. First I ate some hog jowls for breakfast. Then I sat in my rocker and rocked. I rocked all morning. I rocked all afternoon, except for one spell when I had to swat a fly. I rocked all the way up to supper time. Whew! I'm tuckered out. I haven't been that busy in years.*

*B. L.*


*Maggie rang the doorbell and nothing happened. She rang it again, but nothing happened. She rang it once more, and Maggie heard a quiet squeaking noise. Then the door slowly opened. A gray-haired, elderly lady in a wheelchair appeared at the door and asked in a sweet voice, "Yes, can I help you?"   Elise G. - age 11*


## Hands-On Activities

 Get a piece of lined notebook paper. In the margin on the left side, write the hour you woke up yesterday. Example: 7:00. Underneath it, on every line, write the hour that comes next in the day.

Example:   7:00
8:00
9:00
10:00

Continue writing times until every line has a time on it. You should have a vertical row of times in the margin on the left side of the page when you are finished.


Beside each time, write what you did during that hour. If you can't remember, ask a family member to help you recall what you were doing. When you are finished, you will have a sequence of events that happened yesterday.

 Use the sequence of events that you created in the previous

activity to write a narrative paragraph about your day. You don't need to include every single thing you did in every hour. Choose a few big things that happened, and write about those things in the order they occurred.

 Everyone has good days and bad days. Think about the best day you've ever had, or the worst day you've ever had, and write a narrative paragraph telling what happened that made the day wonderful or terrible.

 Do you have a special pet? If so, write a paragraph telling the story of how your pet became a member of the family. If you don't have a pet, ask someone who does have one to share their story, and write it into a narrative paragraph.

# Lesson 14: Persuasive Paragraphs

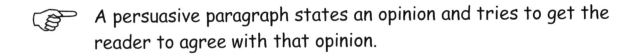

Goal: Write a persuasive paragraph.

## Key Points:

☞ A persuasive paragraph states an opinion and tries to get the reader to agree with that opinion.

☞ A persuasive paragraph usually uses a lot of declarative sentences, but may include imperative sentences and questions as well.

☞ When you write a persuasive paragraph, it's important to know who your audience is so you will know how to persuade them.

☞ A persuasive paragraph paints a picture from a certain point of view so the reader can see it clearly.

## Writing Samples

*Smoking is not a good idea. It is the number one cause of death in the United States, killing 400,000 people each year. Over a quarter of the population smokes even though the percentage decreases each year. Most of them try to quit smoking, but are addicted to the chemicals in smoke. Breathing those substances is bad for your health and can be a nuisance to non-smokers. It seems silly that people smoke cigarettes when you think of what they are made from. As comedian Brad Stine says, "It's just leaves and paper on fire!"*

*George S. - age 13*

*Being an American is a great thing. You have freedom of speech. You have the freedom to live where you want and do what you want to do. Plus, you can get a free education.*

David L. - age 12

*This isn't any old good-for-nothing piece of junk. This is an antique piece of useless junk! It may have been around for hundreds of years. Your forefathers might have had it lying around collecting dust in a shed. George Washington himself might have owned this particular piece of junk. It might even have come over with the Pilgrims on the Mayflower. This isn't just any ordinary useless piece of junk!*

B. L.

## Hands-On Activities

 Salespeople have a tough job. They have to know how to persuade people to buy products. Get together with a family member  or friend, and talk about ways salespeople convince us to buy. What do they do? What do they say? Is there anything they shouldn't do? If you know any salespeople, talk with them about how they persuade people to buy what they are selling.

 Do you have any possessions that you really like, or that are very special to you? Choose one and write a persuasive paragraph to convince people that they need one just like yours.

 What do you like to do in your free time? Do you have a favorite hobby or activity? Write a paragraph that persuades someone else to try your hobby or favorite activity.

Are you proud to be a citizen of your country? If so, write a paragraph persuading others that you live in a great country.

 Do you have something in mind that you would like to receive as a birthday gift? Write a persuasive paragraph letting others know why you should receive this particular gift.

# Lesson 15: Descriptive Paragraphs

## Goal: Write a descriptive paragraph.

### Key Points:

☞ A descriptive paragraph paints a picture so that the reader can feel as though he is experiencing what is happening in the paragraph.

☞ A descriptive paragraph uses a lot of declarative sentences. These may be facts or opinions.

☞ Adjectives are also used in descriptive paragraphs.

☞ When writing a descriptive paragraph, it's important to appeal to the five senses. (See Lesson 2.)

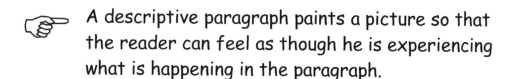

☞ A descriptive paragraph describes something in great detail.

### Writing Samples

*Chicken pot pie is my favorite meal. It has frozen veggies, chopped up potatoes, chunky, crunchy outer crust, thin, moist inner crust, and fresh, soft, juicy meat. I eat it with organic milk as white as snow, and a piece of thick, buttery, chunky Texas toast. For dessert, I have a slice of thick, creamy, dark umber brown chocolate silk pie that melts in your mouth. This is my favorite meal.*

*Kirkpatrick H. - age 10*

*If I had the opportunity to design my own room the way I wanted, it would be cool to the max. It would be big enough to echo when you whisper. I would have tons of electronics, everything from game systems to laptops. A big screen TV would reach from the floor to the ceiling. I would have a surround sound system with tons of subwoofers. The bass would be powerful enough to make the whole room vibrate and feel like a violent thunderstorm is overhead. My windows would overlook a large, slow-flowing river winding through lush green mountains and warm green valleys. The smell of fragrant wildflowers would rush over you from the open windows as you walk through the door. It would be the perfect place to be when you just wanted to be alone and relax, but when you're in the mood to have fun, it could be a happening place. It would have its own private stash of junk food--everything from ice cream to chips and soft drinks. I can almost taste the barbecue chips and the cream soda from my stash.*

*Jared D. - age 13*

*My favorite food is pepperoni pizza. I like my pepperoni pizza with golden brown, thick , puffy crust, and with bold sauce oozing through the snowy mozzarella cheese, topped with blushing red pepperonis. When the pizza comes out of the oven I can smell it a mile away. I like to wait for the pizza to cool so I won't burn my tongue on the hot strings of melted cheese. When I take my first bite I can't describe the wonderful taste in my mouth.*

*Madeline L. - age 12*

## Hands-On Activities

 What is your most favorite meal? Think about that meal and write a paragraph describing it in detail. Instead of simply listing the foods, use your words to help the reader see, smell, and taste the meal.

How would you like to design your own room with an unlimited budget and an unlimited imagination? Write a paragraph that describes your dream room. What do you see? What do you hear? What smells do you detect? How does the room make you feel? Use your observation skills to take the reader there.

 Do you have a hero? A hero doesn't have to be someone who saves the world from evil villains. A hero can be an ordinary person that you know. Write a paragraph describing your hero so that others can understand the qualities that make this person a true hero.

 Look around you and choose one object to describe. Carefully examine the object and write a paragraph describing it in great detail.

# Lesson 16: Journaling

## Goal: Start a journal.

### Key Points:

 A journal is a log where you write your thoughts or other information.

 A journal can be as public or private as you want it to be.

 You can write in your journal daily, or you can write in it more or less often.

 Write often in your journal so that you'll get a lot of writing practice.

Write regularly in your journal so that you won't forget about it.

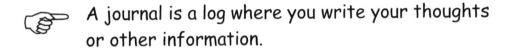

 People keep all kinds of journals, including diaries, nature journals, photo journals, spiritual journals, and historical logs. Many other types of journals exist as well. You can make your journal anything you want it to be.

Journals are a great way to record memories and other information that you don't want to forget. It's fun to go back and read journals you've written in the past.

## Writing Sample

March 21, 2006- Today I went to writing class. After that, I went to the library and got some books and rented a movie. I haven't had a chance to watch it yet, but I hope I will soon.

March 22, 2006- Today I got up and did my schoolwork and P.E. Other than that, nothing very interesting happened, except that my favorite contestant got kicked off of a singing competition show.

March 23, 2006- It's my mom's birthday! Grandma Joanie came over and brought a cake, and it was really good. Later, we went shopping and out to eat. I hope Mom had a good time.

March 24, 2006- Nothing much happened today. I did my schoolwork and then I read for a while. I've been sleepy all day, and it's kind of rainy. It's my cousin Ethan's birthday.

March 25, 2006- It's Saturday, the one day of the week that I get to sleep late, but my dad woke me up at 7:30. I had softball practice. After that I came home and slept.

March 26, 2006- Today is Sunday so I went to church. In the afternoon I watched TV.

March 27, 2006- This is my list of things to do today:
1. Finish schoolwork.
2. Eat lunch.
3. Go to softball practice.
It's my friend Elise's birthday today!

March 28, 2006- Last night I spent the night at Jada's house. Today I'm tired.

*Breanne L. - age 10*

## Hands-On Activities

 Choose a special notebook for a journal. Decide what type of journal you want to keep. Decorate your journal to make it uniquely yours. Decide how often you want to write in it and the type of things you will record. Write your first journal entry.

 As you write in your journal, continue to use the things you learned in these writing lessons, and you will be well on your way to becoming a great writer!

# How to Evaluate Writing
(a section for parents and evaluators)

> The first goal of writing is to build confidence in the writer.

A student who believes he can write will write. It's much more difficult to teach a student who doesn't believe that he can write.

> Praise goes a long ways.

Memorize the rhyme above and make it your motto when evaluating writing.

Approach every paper looking for what is right and good, not for what is wrong.

Always start by listing the strengths of the writing. List them all, every single one that you can find. Find one or two areas that need improvement, and help the writer find ways to remedy those issues.

> Focus on content.

Look for imagination, style, choice of topic, sensory details, supporting evidence--the pillars of great writing!

# Lesson By Lesson Notes and Evaluation

In this section, I will take you lesson by lesson and tell you exactly what to look for as you evaluate your student's work. You'll also receive helpful teaching suggestions.

### Lesson 1: Writing is Communication
The purpose of this lesson is to introduce writing in a non-threatening way. Students are encouraged to use their imaginations and play with words. Keep the lesson fun and lighthearted by participating in the hands-on activities with your student. Allow your student plenty of room for self-expression and only offer suggestions if the student asks for help or if you perceive noticeable frustration. Keep any evaluation to the bare minimum. Just have fun!

### Lesson 2:  Observation Skills
Observation skills are essential to writing. However, if you ask most students to observe a scene and record their findings they will write a list of things they saw and ignore the other senses of hearing, smell, taste, and touch. The exercises in this lesson are designed to help students develop all five senses so they can translate their findings into writing. Your role is to help your student experiment with the different senses using the hands-on activities and expand their observations beyond sight alone.

**Questions for sight exercise:** Make sure the student keeps eyes closed with no peeking and ask the following questions:
1. What am I (the parent/teacher) wearing?
2. What is to your left?
3. What is to your right?
4. What is behind you?
5. What is in front of you?
6. What color is the cover of your writing book?
7. What is the name of your writing curriculum?
8. What color are your best friend's eyes?

**Possible items for smelling exercise:** cinnamon, alcohol, lemon  or citrus fruit, a flower, perfume, soap, garlic, stinky socks

**Suggested items for touch exercise:** cooked noodles, boiled egg, grapes, raisins, rope, rubber gloves, sandpaper, silk, eraser, cotton ball, uncooked pasta, velvet, dough, wax

**Clothing for touch activity:** wool coat, silk scarf or blouse, bathing suit, bathrobe, flannel pajamas, men's dress slacks, raincoat or rubber boots, pantyhose or tights, sequined clothing, fleece jacket, polyester clothing, 100% cotton clothing

## Lesson 3:  Words

The goal of this lesson is to help students recognize the different types of words that are used in writing. Encourage your student to think creatively and use words outside normal, everyday vocabulary.

Answer key for plural noun activity:

| | |
|---|---|
| child-children | ox-oxen |
| mouse-mice | foot-feet |
| goose- geese | mongoose-mongooses |
| tooth-teeth | man-men |
| woman-women | sheep-sheep |
| deer-deer | moose-moose |
| baby-babies | city-cities |
| potato-potatoes | hero-heroes |
| box-boxes | life-lives |
| half-halves | loaf-loaves |
| wolf- wolves | person-people |
| cactus-cacti | |

Fill in the blanks exercise

*Paragraph #1*

I have a new pet.  It's a _____ _____.  My pet likes
                          *adjective*    *noun*

to _____ and it eats _____ _____ very _____.
   *verb*                *adjective* *plural noun*      *adverb*

It lives in a _____ in my _____.  My pet is very _____
             *noun*           *noun*                        *adjective*

67

and that's why I named it _____.   I love my new pet
                           *proper noun (name)*

because it is so _____.
                    *adjective*

*Paragraph # 2*

My very favorite snack is _____ _____ served with
                              *adjective*      *noun*

_____ _____.  I like to twirl it around on my fork, plop it in my
*adjective  plural noun*

mouth and chew very _____.   It's even good for me and builds
                          *adverb*

strong _____ and _____. I call my snack _____
      *plural noun*      *plural noun*                  *proper noun*

because it tastes so _____.
                       *adjective*

## Lesson 4:  Basic Sentence Structure

It's time to string words together into sentences. It may take a while for your student to grasp the concept that every sentence is a complete thought with at least two parts: a subject and a verb. To help your student determine whether or not the thought is complete, ask the following questions:
1. Who or what is doing something?
2. What action was taken? Sometimes the subject doesn't take action, but is simply being. For example: Patrick is nice. In this case, ask your student what Patrick is being.

Now is the time to teach your student to capitalize the first word of every sentence and provide punctuation at the end. It's best to develop and enforce this habit now while your student is learning to write sentences so that it will come naturally in the future.

Answers to the sentence fragment and run-on sentence activities will vary. Please be sure every sentence has both a subject and a verb.

Answers to the word rearrangement activity:

| the | speedy | red | race | car | chased | the | yellow | convertible | sports | car |
|-----|--------|-----|------|-----|--------|-----|--------|-------------|--------|-----|

1. The speedy red race car chased the yellow convertible sports car.
2. The red speedy race car chased the yellow convertible sports car.
3. The speedy red race car chased the convertible yellow sports car.
4. The speedy red race car chased the yellow sports car convertible.
5. The red speedy race car chased the convertible yellow sports car.
6. The red speedy race car chased the yellow sports car convertible.
7. The yellow speedy race car chased the red convertible sports car.
8. The speedy yellow race car chased the convertible red sports car.
9. The yellow speedy race car chased the convertible red sports car.
10. The yellow speedy race car chased he red sports car convertible.
11. The speedy yellow race car chased the red convertible sports car.
12. The speedy yellow race car chased the red sports car convertible.
13. The red convertible race car chased the speedy yellow sports car.
14. The convertible red race car chased the speedy yellow sports car.
15. The red race car convertible chased the speedy yellow sports car.
16. The yellow convertible race car chased the speedy red sports car.
17. The convertible yellow race car chased the speedy red sports car.
18. The yellow race car convertible chased the speedy red sports car.
19. The red convertible race car chased the yellow speedy sports car.
20. The convertible red race car chased the yellow speedy sports car.
21. The red race car convertible chased the yellow speedy sports car.
22. The yellow convertible race car chased the red speedy sports car.
23. The convertible yellow race car chased the red speedy sports car.
24. The yellow race car convertible chased the red speedy sports car.
25. The speedy red sports car chased the yellow convertible race car.
26. The red speedy sports car chased the yellow convertible race car.
27. The speedy red sports car chased the convertible yellow race car.
28. The speedy red sports car chased the yellow race car convertible.
29. The red speedy sports car chased the convertible yellow race car.
30. The red speedy sports car chased the yellow race car convertible.

31. The yellow speedy sports car chased the red convertible race car.
32. The speedy yellow sports car chased the convertible red race car.
33. The yellow speedy sports car chased the convertible red race car.
34. The yellow speedy sports car chased the red race car convertible.
35. The speedy yellow sports car chased the red convertible race car.
36. The speedy yellow sports car chased the red race car convertible.
37. The red convertible sports car chased the speedy yellow race car.
38. The convertible red sports car chased the speedy yellow race car.
39. The red sports car convertible chased the speedy yellow race car.
40. The yellow convertible sports car chased the speedy red race car.
41. The convertible yellow sports car chased the speedy red race car.
42. The yellow sports car convertible chased the speedy red race car.
43. The red convertible sports car chased the yellow speedy race car.
44. The convertible red sports car chased the yellow speedy race car.
45. The red sports car convertible chased the yellow speedy race car.
46. The yellow convertible sports car chased the red speedy race car.
47. The convertible yellow sports car chased the red speedy race car.
48. The yellow sports car convertible chased the red speedy race car.

Answer key for paragraph:

Dogs make great pets. You can train them to do tricks. They can go on walks with you. They guard your house. Dogs are loyal to their owners. A dog is a man's best friend.

## Lesson 5: Declarative Sentences

Declarative sentences make a statement. When evaluating your student's declarative sentences, be sure that the sentences don't ask a question, express strong emotion, or give a command.

## Lesson 6: Imperative Sentences

Imperative sentences give a command or tell someone to do something. When evaluating your student's imperative sentences make sure that the sentences don't ask a question or make a statement. Each sentence should tell someone to do something.

## Lesson 7: Interrogative Sentences

Interrogative sentences ask a question. When evaluating your student's work make sure that each interrogative sentence is, indeed, a question and that each one ends with a question mark.

## Lesson 8: Exclamatory Sentences

An exclamatory sentence should express excitement or strong emotion, but should not give a command. For instance, the following sentence expresses strong emotion and ends with an exclamation point, but it is actually an imperative sentence because it tells someone to do something: *Help me!* Whereas, an exclamatory sentence is a statement. Example: *The circus is so much fun!*

Also, make sure that your student hasn't written an interjection, which is one word that expresses strong emotion. Example: *Ouch!*

Each exclamatory sentence should end with an exclamation point.

## Lesson 9: Paragraph Formation

In this first lesson on paragraphs make sure the student's paragraph is indented and focuses on one subject, the newly discovered island. Point out any sentences that stray from the topic of the island.

If a student is having difficulty writing several sentences about the topic, be prepared to jumpstart the process with a few questions:

Where is your island?          What animals live there?
What plants grow there?          What is the weather like?
What does your island look like?

## Lesson 10: The Topic Sentence

If your student has trouble writing a topic sentence, explore the subject orally first. Ask your student questions about the topic to help decipher what point he is trying to make in a particular paragraph. Keep asking questions until the topic is narrow enough for a single paragraph and help the student formulate his thoughts into one sentence.

Possible topic sentence for paragraphs.

Paragraph #1:
You can find a shooting star.
A shooting star is easy to see.

Paragraph # 2
Skydiving is easy.
I can tell you how to skydive.

Paragraph # 3
The circus is a great show.
I really like the circus.

## Lesson 11: Supporting Sentences

Once your student has a topic sentence, walk him through these questions to determine what other sentences need to be in the paragraph.

Who?
What?
When?
Where?
How?
Why?

who what
when where
why how

## Lesson 12: Expository Paragraphs

An expository paragraph gives information.
Sometimes it can define, instruct, explain, or clarify,

but the essence of the paragraph is simply offering information to the reader. Before evaluating your student's expository paragraphs, read the assignment listed in the hands-on activities section to see if the student is asked to give information, explain, instruct, define, or clarify. When you evaluate the paragraphs, make sure the student has carried out the specific instruction for each paragraph.

Check to be sure the paragraph is indented, has a clear topic sentence, and the supporting sentences remain on topic without straying.

## Lesson 13:  Narrative Paragraphs

A narrative paragraph tells a very short story or a portion of a story. It doesn't simply give information, but records a series of events. When evaluating narrative paragraphs, make sure the sequence of events are in the correct order and any information crucial to understanding the story is present and hasn't been omitted.

> **First**
> **Second**
> **Third**

Check to make sure the paragraph is indented, has a clear topic sentence, and the supporting sentences remain on topic without straying.

## Lesson 14: Persuasive Paragraphs

In order to convince someone of something, we have to be convinced ourselves. It's important that in each persuasive paragraph the student has a clear, confident opinion and doesn't sound wishy-washy.

It's also important that the student writes with a particular audience in mind. This will help the student to formulate specific ideas that will convince that particular audience to agree with his or her opinion. For each paragraph assigned in the hands-on activities, ask your student who the audience will be and discuss ways to convince that particular audience.

Sometimes students have difficulty determining a specific audience and want to write for everyone. In that case, ask your student questions that will help him or her focus on a much smaller group of people or a particular individual. For example, if the student is persuading someone to get him or her a special birthday gift you might ask questions like: Who normally gives you birthday gifts? Who would be most likely to give this particular gift and why? Who do you want to receive this gift from? Who can afford to buy this gift for you?

Check to make sure each paragraph is indented, has a clear topic sentence, and the supporting sentences remain on topic without straying.

## Lesson 15: Descriptive Paragraphs

Descriptive paragraphs paint a picture for the reader. They also appeal to the five senses, but most students have a tendency to concentrate only on the sense of sight. In order to help your student overcome this tendency, ask questions when evaluating descriptive paragraphs. For example, if the student describes an object you might prompt with questions like: What does it look like? Can you compare it to any other object? Does it make a sound? Does the object have an odor? What does it feel like when you touch it? Is it sour or sweet? (If taste is applicable to the object being described).

Check to make sure each paragraph is indented, has a clear topic sentence, and the supporting sentences remain on topic without straying.

## Lesson 16: Journaling

At this point, your student has learned the basics of writing and is ready to move to larger writing projects.

A great way to transition to longer pieces is by journaling.

Help your student decide what type of journal he or she would like to keep. Make sure the choice reflects the student's personality and interests. Choose an appropriate journal (three ring notebook, composition notebook, diary, etc...). Encourage the student to decorate the journal and take ownership of it.

Plan together how often the student will write in the journal. It's easy to start a new journal, but consistently writing in it may be a challenge. You will likely need to help your student set specific times or dates to write in it and you'll need to follow through to make sure the writing is accomplished. Allow the student as much input as possible into these decisions, but check regularly to make sure writing is happening.

One of the best ways to encourage students to write is to model the behavior. As your student starts journaling, consider starting your own journal as well. You might even start a journal together with both of you contributing to it regularly. Teamwork always makes the load seem lighter.

Your student has worked hard to master some of the most basic writing skills in this curriculum. Don't forget to celebrate that accomplishment!

# Proofreading Checklist

Each time you write, use this checklist to proofread your work before you turn it in to your parent or teacher.

1. Did I do my best work?

2. Is my handwriting neat and easy to read?

3. Have I written complete sentences?

4. Do all of my sentences begin with a capital letter and end with a punctuation mark?

5. Did I indent paragraphs?

6. Did I check the spelling of any words I wasn't sure how to spell?

# More writing resources by Bonita Lillie

## *Fun Foundations in Writing II: Communicating with Others*
(coming in 2014)

Continue the writing fun with the second book in the *Fun Foundations in Writing* series. Use the skills you've already learned to write longer, even more fun works of writing.

## *Hands-On Essays*

*Hands-On Essays* is written for middle and high school students who are ready for a bigger writing challenge. The curriculum walks students step-by-step through the process of mastering the essay and even includes FREE instructional video lessons taught by the author! Visit www.handsonessays.com for more information.

## *Bonita Lillie's Writing Tips*

Enjoy a newsletter full of writing tips and ideas delivered right to your inbox every two weeks! Sign up at www.bonitalillie.com.